Not in Otter's Pocket

Written by Suzanne Senior

Illustrated by Angelika Scudamore

Collins

Sea Otter had a smooth, grey stone.
He twirled it in his paws.

He threw it high and caught it.

He kept it safe in his armpit pocket.

"It's the best stone in the world!" he said.

One day, Otter went swimming.

He leapt and dived and floated.

Then he peered in his pocket.

"My stone is not here!" he exclaimed.
"I wonder where it is."

Otter searched all over the beach.
The stone was not there.

He scooped up a new stone.
It was the right size.

Oh dear!

It was not a stone. It was a crab!

"Ouch!" yelled Otter. "This has claws."

Otter looked stern.

"I don't want claws in my pocket," he said.

Otter poked around in some seaweed.

He saw a bright blue stone.

Oh dear!

It was not a stone. It was an urchin!
Otter squeaked, "This has spikes!"

He frowned and put it down.

"I don't want spikes in my pocket,"
he complained.

Next, Otter peered into a pool.

He found a small, brown stone.

Oh dear!

It was not a stone. It was a sea snail!
Otter gasped, "This makes slime!"

He set the snail free.

"I don't want slime in my pocket,"
he groaned.

Otter wiped away a tear.

Then, he saw something ...

"My old stone!" cheered Otter.

He started twirling it in his paws.
He threw it high and caught it.

He tucked it into his armpit pouch.

"It's the best stone in the world!" he said.

What Otter found

After reading

Letters and Sounds: Phase 5

Word count: 250

Focus phonemes: /igh/ i, i-e /ai/ ay, ey /oa/ o, o-e /oo/ ue, ew /ow/ ou /ee/ ea /ar/ a /or/ aw, augh, al /air/ ere /ur/ ir, or, ear /ear/ ere, eer /e/ ea /o/ a /u/ o-e

Common exception words: the, into, put, my, he, said, one, where, oh

Curriculum links: Animals, including humans

National Curriculum learning objectives: Reading/word reading: read other words of more than one syllable that contain taught GPCs; Reading/comprehension: understand both the books they can already read accurately and fluently and those they listen to by checking that the text makes sense to them as they read, and correcting inaccurate reading

Developing fluency

- Your child may enjoy hearing you read the book.
- Each take the part of the narrator or Otter. Encourage lots of expression to add drama to the story.

Phonic practice

- Look together at pages 2 and 3. Ask your child to find the two words that contain the /ur/ sound. (twirled, world) Point out that the spellings are different. (ir, or)
- Repeat the challenge for the following pages:
  - On page 2, find two words that contain the /oo/ sound. (**smooth, threw**)
  - On page 4, find two words that contain the /e/ sound. (**went, leapt**)
- Challenge your child to find words with matching sounds with different spellings.

Extending vocabulary

- Look together at page 9 and ask your child to mime Otter looking **stern**. Ask: Can you think of a synonym for **stern**? (e.g. *cross, grumpy*)
- Look together at the following words and, after your child has mimed the focus word, ask them to suggest a synonym:
  - Page 14: **peered** (e.g. *peeped, looked, spied*)
  - Page 18: **wiped** (e.g. *cleaned, dried*)
  - Page 20: **twirling** (e.g. *spinning, turning, twisting*)